SCALING TIME VS WEALTH

AN INVESTOR'S
GUIDE TO

SCALING
WEALTH ~~WEALTH~~
TIME

How to Break Free From the Grind & Turn
Financial Success into Choices, Options and
a Life of Fulfillment

DR. DAVID PHELPS, DDS

Scaling Your Wealth: How to Break Free From the Grind & Turn Financial Success into Choices, Options a Life of Fulfillment

Copyright ©2024 DPI Media, LLC

All Rights Reserved. No part of this publication may be reproduced, stored in a retrieval system, or transmitted, in any form or by any means, electronic, mechanical, photocopying, recording, or otherwise, without the prior written permission of the copyright holder. Printed in the United States of America.

For information, address David Phelps International LLC, 519 E. IH 30 Suite 246, Rockwall, TX 75087

Cover Design by Monica Austin, Mocah Studios, LLC
Cartoons licensed by CartoonStock.com. Used with Permission.

ISBN: 979-8-218-58967-7 (paperback)

First printing: January 2025

TABLE OF CONTENTS

INTRODUCTION xi
Does Time Equal Money or Money Equal Time? ....*xi*
Money is Tokenized Time ....*xi*
From Money to Freedom ....*xii*
The End Goal: More Time, Not More Money ....*xiv*
Challenging the Grind Culture ....*xiv*
Designing Life to Support Freedom ....*xv*

Price of Time vs. Value of Wealth 1
The American Dream - As Defined By Whom? *2*
The Time Value of Money vs. The Value of Time *4*
Sitting Crushed at the Airport *6*
True Wealth Lies in Time Freedom *8*

The Evolution to Freedom 11
*Progressing From Trading Time for Dollars
to Acquiring Asset Based Income* *11*
Asset Based Accumulation vs Accumulation *15*

The Grind Isn't The Goal 17
Be Wary of Glorifying the Wrong Metrics *19*
Are you optimizing for income or for time? *20*
Freedom While You Are Still Young Enough to Enjoy It ... *21*
Redefining Success: From Hustle to Fulfillment *23*

Cashflow is King 25
The Importance of Balancing Equity and Cash Flow *28*
Cash Flow Producing Assets: The Key to Freedom *28*

Why the Accumulation Mindset Keeps You Stuck *29*
The Freedom-Focused Model *30*

Breaking the Cycle 33

Strategies for Scaling Time *33*
Freedom vs Efficiency *34*
Clarifying Decisions *34*
Delegation - A Hidden Superpower *36*
How To Utilize an Executive Assistant *36*
Best Practices for an Executive Assistant *38*

The Power of Clarity & Focus 41

Defining Your Freedom Number *41*
Linking Freedom to Personal Values *42*
Strategic Use of Assets for Passive Income *43*
Leveraging Technology for Financial Clarity *45*
Dealing with Setbacks and Adjusting Your Freedom Number *46*

Freedom is Just the Beginning 49

Time as the Ultimate Asset *49*
Reflections on the Journey to Financial Independence *50*
Leveraging Financial Strategies for Time Freedom *51*
The Legacy of Time Freedom *53*
AFTERWORD: *57*
What Is Freedom Founders? *57*
A PRACTICE OWNER TURNED CEO AND LEADER *63*

*To my Freedom Founders Tribe:
A community of colleagues who are living these principles
and showing the world what it looks like to live free.
You inspire me!*

INTRODUCTION

Does Time Equal Money or Does Money Equal Time?

This is not a practical "how to" on time management. It is a new philosophy on how to think about wealth. In this book, I'll share some life changing principles that I have discovered through evaluating time as an asset and using financial principles to understand a better way of evaluating the balance sheet of our lives. These are lessons learned through working with hundreds of practice professionals who, by society's standards, would be considered extremely successful, but who find themselves feeling trapped, dissatisfied and looking for more.

In later chapters, I will share some strategies that have helped myself and many of my colleagues translate "success" into more autonomy, choices and options in their lives.

Money is Tokenized Time

There is a modern cliché that says, "time is money." But is that really true?

I prefer George Gilder's phrase, "money is tokenized time." Gilder believed there to be a connection between money and human productivity. Money represents the value created through human effort and ingenuity. As people work and produce, they contribute their time and skills, which are compensated with money. In this way, money allows individuals to trade their time for the goods and services they desire.

However, money is not just a medium of exchange—it reflects the energy and time invested by individuals. Understanding this concept of money as tokenized time challenges the conventional view of the pursuit of wealth is merely an effort to accumulate money.

Our society tends to honor those who more aggressively tokenize their time. Why is that? What would change if you were to reverse that assumption and begin utilizing money as a means of acquiring time as an asset?

To put it in Gilder's words, is tokenizing your time into money really accomplishing true success?

If wealth were measured by the currency of time, how wealthy is your personal balance sheet?

What if the default assumption that "time is money" is actually backwards?

> **What if the default assumption that "time is money" is actually backwards?**

From Money to Freedom

Early in life, the majority focus on earning money to make ends meet. As time passes, the goal shifts to financial stability and maintaining a comfortable lifestyle. This traditional path, often modelled for us and implicitly expected of us by society, keeps many locked in a cycle of working to support their families and lifestyles. But what happens when you no longer want to spend most of your time working? When the desire to be present for your family or pursue other avenues of personal fulfillment takes over?

As time passes, the question becomes more urgent: Is wealth really about more money, or is it about the ability to control and take ownership of your time? Most people don't realize until it's too late that what they truly want is not more financial accumulation, but more freedom—freedom to choose how to spend their time.

"I wouldn't worry about going before your time. You're too old to die young."

The key question is: how do we make the best use of our time right now, instead of deferring our happiness and fulfillment to some distant future?

The End Goal: More Time, Not More Money

What most truly want in life is more freedom of time. This doesn't necessarily mean "retirement" (the origins of the word retirement means "to be removed from service"). Nor does it mean quitting activities that provide purpose. It means having the choice to spend your time in ways that bring you joy. It means breaking free from the cycle of working because you feel you *have* to, and instead doing what you love because you *want* to.

Many people continue in work they dislike, burnt out from years of doing the same thing, even if it provides financial stability. The fear of having to keep grinding until the average retirement age of 65 or 70 weighs heavily on them. But true freedom is the ability to design a life that fits you, one where you control your time rather than letting societal expectations dictate it.

Challenging the Grind Culture

Many entrepreneurs tie their self-worth to the amount of time they spend working. They equate long hours to a strong work ethic. The longer and harder they work, they believe, the bigger and better the results. But this couldn't be further from the truth. Long hours and endless hustle might result in financial gain, but they often come at the cost of personal fulfillment, relationships, and health.

Entrepreneurs and professionals who brag about how hard

they work are often out of balance—mentally, physically, spiritually, and financially. Success should not be defined by the hours spent on the business, but by the freedom it provides to enjoy life. You're not in business to run a business. You're in business to create **freedom**—the freedom to do what you want, when you want, where you want, and with whom you want.

Designing Life to Support Freedom

I've had the incredible opportunity to work closely with hundreds of business and professional practice owners and their partners—whether a spouse, significant other, or both—as they define their vision of freedom. Time, as it turns out, is always at the heart of these conversations. Almost without exception, I've found that these couples are far closer than they realize to having the freedom to create more time for the people, experiences, and memories that truly matter—those things that often feel like they're slipping away.

So, what's holding them back? It's not a lack of resources or opportunities—it's a lack of clarity. A lack of focus. And most importantly, the absence of a plan that allows both voices to be heard, validated, and united. Too often, they're stuck because they can't see how to bridge the gap without undoing what they've already built or risking financial stability.

> *Too often, they're stuck because they can't see how to bridge the gap without undoing what they've already built or risking financial stability.*

The solution? A plan designed not just to spark change but to drive transformation—real, lasting transformation. And the results? Life-changing. The stories from the Freedom Founders Community are proof of what's possible. These aren't just tales of financial breakthroughs; they're stories of rediscovered time, deeper connections, and lives reimagined. Each one is a testament to the power of aligning goals and taking intentional steps forward.

In the next few chapters I will invite you to challenge some of the basic assumptions that society engrains in us about money, time, and how we define success. We'll take a close look at our time balance sheet and see our net worth through a different lens.

We'll address some key questions:

- How does your relationship with money align with your life goals?
- Are you using money merely as a tool for survival, or as a means of creating true wealth?
- If money could grant you the freedom to design your life on your own terms, how would that change the choices you make today?

Is true wealth the accumulation of money, or is it the acquisition of time and freedom? More importantly, are you actively building a life that reflects this understanding, or are you still tethered to a cycle that prioritizes income over autonomy? The answers may hold the key to not just financial freedom, but a life where money fuels purpose, fulfillment, and choice.

CHAPTER ONE

The Price of Time vs. The Value of Wealth

Is your time worth more today or in the future?

Time is a currency—a value exchange system. Just as we budget our money, we should budget our time. It can be spent, saved, invested, or squandered. Unlike money, however, time is finite and non-renewable. Every moment spent cannot be reclaimed, making time more valuable than any amount of money.

The question is: What is the price of time? Do we sacrifice time today in the hope that it will be worth more in the future? Do we value our current relationships less because we believe the future holds more promise? Far too often, we get trapped in this way of thinking. When you spend money to buy something, you are really paying for that purchase with your time - the time you spent to earn that money, and more importantly, the future time Freedom that money could buy.

Think about how much of your time is taken from you each year—through taxes, inflation, and the relentless chase for financial success. Back to Gilder's premise: If money is tokenized time, how much of your time is spent just producing the taxes and expenses imposed on you by the system? And how much more is sacrificed in the name of pursuing wealth?

The American Dream - As Defined By Whom?

Everyone starts out in life trading their time for dollars to pay the bills and enhance their lifestyle. There's nothing inherently wrong with that—it's where I started too. But building more wealth typically just leads to spending more on lifestyle. There is nothing wrong with enjoying nice things and providing a certain lifestyle for yourself and your family. But understand that there is a universal law of nature - without intention, that lifestyle will expand, and you will find yourself chasing a vision of success that's constantly moving farther away.

So, what do we really want in life?

The American ideal of success has long been built around ambition, wealth, and status. We glorify stories of rags to riches, of climbing the corporate ladder, of obtaining higher salaries and better offices with bigger views. Yet, this pursuit of wealth often comes at the cost of what truly matters—our time, relationships, and personal fulfillment.

The truth is, success isn't about accumulating dollars. True success is about life satisfaction-having the freedom to spend your time on what brings you joy and nurturing the relationships that mean the most. But society rarely measures those things, and that's where we lose sight of what really counts.

This disconnect between wealth and well-being isn't just anecdotal—it's backed by research. The Easterlin Paradox

shows that while wealthier individuals tend to report higher life satisfaction than those with less, increasing a country's overall wealth doesn't lead to a corresponding rise in happiness.[1] In other words, as societies grow richer, collective happiness doesn't necessarily improve. The World Happiness Report supports this further, ranking the happiest countries based on factors like social support, work-life balance, and personal freedom—not income levels. Countries like Finland and Denmark consistently top the list, not because they chase endless wealth, but because they prioritize well-being over financial accumulation.[2]

Today, the idea of success is shifting. It's no longer just about accumulating wealth or climbing the corporate ladder. More and more people are redefining success to focus on balance, relationships, health, and time freedom.

After the Covid pandemic of 2020, unprecedented numbers of workers left their jobs, rethinking their lives and the lack of purpose that had left them feeling void and empty. Fifty million Americans renounced their jobs, and another third of the workforce is renegotiating when, where, and how they will work. The wake-up call of mortality and the reevaluation of what truly matters has led many to search for meaning and significance, rejecting the old definitions of success and the long-accepted American Dream. In a world where wealth is no longer the only measure, we must ask ourselves: What truly holds value?

The Time Value of Money vs. The Value of Time

In finance, the Time Value of Money (TVM) is a principle that states that a sum of money in the hand today is worth more than the same sum to be paid in the future. People are willing to pay interest on money because having it today means it can be reinvested to generate more value over time.

If I invest my savings today, I expect to receive my original investment back plus a return. But this principle, while crucial in finance, is rarely applied to my valuable currencies, such as our time. While money can be reinvested to grow, time is finite. Once spent, it's gone forever.

This makes the value of time fundamentally different from the value of money. Time is the ultimate currency—something that cannot be earned back or multiplied once spent. The relentless pursuit of wealth often leads us to sacrifice time, believing we'll make it up later. But what if time today is more valuable than wealth tomorrow?

> **What if time today is more valuable than wealth tomorrow?**

Many people spend their entire lives accumulating financial assets in the hope of buying freedom later. But the problem is that time spent today—on relationships, passions, and well-being—can't be reclaimed with money tomorrow. I learned this lesson firsthand.

It wasn't until my daughter's health crisis that I realized the true cost of chasing financial security. I finally understood that what I really needed was more time with the people I loved.

My Moment of Truth

My wake-up call didn't come from a pandemic like so many others. It came from my daughter's battle for survival. Already a survivor of leukemia and epileptic seizures, Jenna, at just 12 years old, was in end-stage liver failure. By the grace of God and the selflessness of a family who donated their daughter's organs after a tragic accident, Jenna received a life-saving liver transplant, giving her—and me—a second chance.

I also received the grace of a second chance—a chance to reevaluate my priorities. I've always been driven, setting goals and persevering until they're achieved. But I had to ask myself: to what end? What was the destination? How was I measuring success?

It became clear that I didn't need more income, a higher hourly production, or a greater offer on a practice buyout. I needed time. I needed freedom over my time. I needed to convert the value or equity I had created into tokenized time—time to spend with my daughter before it was too late.

Fortunately, I had learned to acquire tangible assets like real estate early on, before becoming a dentist. Those assets produced a steady stream of income that allowed me to stop trading my time for money. I "had enough" passive income to buy back my time—at least for a year or two. And that's exactly what I did.

Sitting Crushed at the Airport

Andy was a successful oral surgeon, a role that provided well for his family but demanded a high cost. His career, though lucrative, came with a trade-off: the income flowed only as long as his hands were busy. Not only that, but as an oral surgeon he found his most profitable months were over the summer or during spring break, what Andy dubbed "The Super Bowl" of oral surgery. Andy's life slowly oriented toward being most busy at work when his kids were out of school.

Over time, he began feeling the strain of this exchange. The steady pressure to keep up—both financially and professionally—was wearing him down, and the life he'd built started to feel like a trap. In March of 2018, he found himself at Gate 5 of Northwest Arkansas International Airport, waiting to catch a flight to yet another implant training course. But this time was different. This time, his stomach was in knots. Next week would be spring break, usually one of his busiest and most profitable weeks at the practice, but it was also a chance for his wife and son to go skiing in Colorado with their friends. While his family was headed to the slopes, he was headed back into the grind. It was the life he had chosen, yet the regret he felt was undeniable. He would miss out on creating memories with his family, memories that could never be recreated. There were no do-overs. Only now.

Staring out the large glass windows at the jets hurtling through the skies, that moment was a visceral reality check. It was time for a change.

> **Staring out the large glass windows at the jets hurtling through the skies, that moment was a visceral reality check. It was time for a change.**

If he wanted to be there for his family, he needed to create more freedom over his time, not just his income. It was the beginning of his real journey to freedom—a freedom that would allow him to prioritize moments that truly mattered. Fast forward to 2021, and Andy's life had changed in a way he hadn't thought possible. He had created enough passive income to take the entire spring break off with his family. This time, he didn't feel torn or anxious about missed revenue. Instead, he was fully present on the ski slopes, finally realizing that time—not income—is the true measure of wealth. His son and daughter would only have a handful of spring breaks left before they left home, and Andy was determined to make the most of every one. As one of my good friends often says about his children, "you only get 18 summers."

> **As one of my good friends often says about his children, "you only get 18 summers."**

Andy's journey illustrates a truth we often overlook: while financial success is valuable, it pales in comparison to the freedom of time. We might be tempted to chase wealth endlessly, but time is irreplaceable—an asset that, once spent, is gone forever.

True Wealth Lies in Time Freedom

Financial wealth can be accumulated and stored for later use, time cannot. You never truly know for certain how much time you will be given. Every moment is a gift.

Instead of working endlessly in the hope of retiring later, imagine designing a life where you have the Freedom to enjoy the gift of time today. This might mean reducing your workload, investing in systems or assets that generate passive income, or setting clearer boundaries between work and personal time.

My recommendation? Achieve meaningful autonomy over

your time now, while you are still young enough to enjoy it.

In the following chapters, we'll explore what it looks like to evolve toward Freedom through smart financial choices and lifestyle changes.

Footnote/Endnote Citing Sources

[1] Richard A. Easterlin, "Does Economic Growth Improve the Human Lot? Some Empirical Evidence," Nations and Households in Economic Growth, Academic Press, 1974.

[2] Helliwell, J., Layard, R., & Sachs, J. (Eds.), World Happiness Report 2021, Sustainable Development Solutions Network, 2021.

SCALING TIME VS WEALTH

CHAPTER TWO

The Evolution to Freedom

Progressing From Trading Time for Dollars to Acquiring Asset Based Income

Every journey toward financial freedom begins with understanding where you are today and defining where you ultimately want to go. In the beginning, we all start out needing to earn money, trading our time for dollars to pay the bills and improve our lifestyle. This is a necessary phase of life, but it's important to recognize this as a starting point. True freedom comes when you move beyond this stage.

This will require progressing from being a technical worker to becoming a business owner, where you leverage systems and people to reduce your reliance on active income. Ultimately, the journey leads to becoming an investor, where your assets generate passive income, buying back your time. This evolution from worker to owner to investor is the key to reclaiming your time and achieving lasting financial freedom.

The Technical Worker

In the first stage of this journey, you start as a technical worker. You have degrees, education, and licenses. You enter the workforce or start your own business, applying your skills in exchange for a paycheck. You're trading your time for money.

This is where most of us begin. I started here as well. But the ultimate goal is to evolve beyond this as quickly as possible. You don't want to spend your whole life trading time for dollars. As your income increases, so too do the demands on your time. The more you earn, the more responsibility you take on, leaving you with less time to enjoy the life you're working so hard to build.

The Business Operator

The next step is becoming a business operator. You can still apply your technical skills, but now you're also responsible for owning and running the business. However, at this stage, the business often still owns you. You're not just providing technical skills—you're also managing day-to-day operations, which can feel like a never-ending grind.

I recently spoke with a pediatric dentist who's doing well by traditional standards—he runs a successful practice, yet he's working 60-plus hours a week while raising young daughters. He feels trapped, constantly working long hours because he believes that's the only way to succeed. He doesn't know how to break free from the hamster wheel, but he's starting to realize that there must be another way.

Working harder and faster is not the answer. The key is to put systems and people in place to run the day-to-day operations, giving you the freedom to step away.

You're not in business to simply run a business—you're in business to create freedom. The freedom to do what you want, when you want, with whomever you want.

Your business should support your life, not the other way around. Too many people get stuck thinking they own the business when, in reality, the business owns them. Don't stop at this stage.

> **Your business should support your life, not the other way around.**

The True Business Owner

The next step is becoming a true business owner. This is where you've elevated yourself to the point where the business can run without your constant involvement. You may still participate in high-level decisions or meetings, but you now have the freedom to step away, travel, and focus on working on the business rather than in it.

One of the most important skills in this stage is learning how to market your products or services effectively. Unfortunately, marketing is often overlooked or misunderstood by small business owners. If more business owners mastered marketing, their businesses would not only be more profitable but would also free up their time faster.

The Investor

The final stage in the journey to true freedom is becoming an investor. As an investor, your money is working for you. You're investing in other businesses or assets that generate passive income, freeing you from the need to actively work. You're partnering with others to reap the benefits of those investments, and this represents the pinnacle of financial independence—a level I truly enjoy being at.

This is where true freedom is realized. You've moved beyond being tied to a job or business and now rely on the income your investments generate. Whether through businesses, real estate, or other tangible assets, you are no longer tied to trading time for money.

> *This is where true freedom is realized. You've moved beyond being tied to a job and now rely on the income your investments generate.*

That said, you can still engage in the work you love if you choose to. If you're passionate about your field, there's no reason to abandon it. But understanding how to operate a real business, market effectively, and invest in other people and assets brings broad diversification. By diversifying across multiple businesses, real estate, and investments, you ensure you're not putting all your eggs in one basket.

Reaching the investor stage requires a long-term mindset. You need to focus on building and growing assets over time, which will ultimately grant you the financial independence and time freedom you desire.

The key is to replace your active income with passive income, generated from assets that require far less time to manage. Your primary business is an asset, but it demands a lot of your time to remain profitable. This isn't true freedom. By reinvesting your active income into other assets—businesses, real estate, or other ventures—you can begin to shift from working for money to having your money work for you.

Asset Based Income vs Accumulation

The traditional "retirement" models offered by most financial advisors focuses primarily on accumulation vs the acquisition of cash flow producing assets which are capable of generating sustainable replacement income.

This leaves many professionals with a theoretical "net worth" that is not particularly useful in creating meaningful autonomy over how they spend their time.

> **This leaves many professionals with a theoretical "net worth" that is not particularly useful in creating meaningful autonomy over how they spend their time.**

To achieve true time freedom, you need to define your freedom number—the amount of passive income required to live comfortably without relying on active work. Once you hit this number, you can step away from the daily grind, knowing that your income will continue to support your lifestyle.

Unlike traditional savings models, where you stash money away in a 401k or savings account, this approach focuses on assets that generate income. You're not simply accumulating wealth—you're putting it to work. And when that income begins to replace your active income, you're on your way to true freedom.

We'll discuss this more in subsequent chapters.

The path to financial freedom is a journey—from being a worker to a business owner and ultimately becoming an investor. Each stage builds on the last, but the real key to reducing dependence on trading time for earned income lies in understanding the power of passive income. The goal should be to replace your reliance on earned income as quickly as possible. By focusing on building assets that generate income without your active involvement and defining your freedom number, you can fast-track your journey and reclaim your time.

CHAPTER THREE

The Grind Isn't The Goal

Breaking Free From Society's "Hustle & Grind" Trap

A few years ago at a major dental conference I was approached by a young dentist who was highly motivated and success oriented. He proudly shared his personal goal of reaching a $50M net worth over the next few years.

"Why $50M?" I asked.

He seemed surprised by my question, and gave a vague answer about building a family legacy.

"Let me ask you a question," I replied. "Do you think your kids want more money, or do they want more of you?"

What followed was a heartfelt conversation about what really mattered in this young doctor's life.

The more I work with practice professionals, the more I have come to see just how deep certain paradigms are embedded into our philosophy from the beginning. Few fully understand or appreciate how much affect these paradigms can have on the choices we have made that brought us to where we are today.

From a young age, many of us were taught that we can achieve anything if we work hard enough. Our parents, teachers, and other authority figures—well-meaning people—encouraged us to put in extra effort, give 110%, and believe that success would follow. Whether in school, sports, or early career stages, the message was always the same: work hard, and you will succeed.

This is not without merit.

For me, that ethos was essential for surviving the rigors of dental school and the challenges of establishing myself in practice. It was very beneficial in helping me reach a certain measure of stability and the ability to generate a larger than average income. This is good, to a point. But the problem is that it can only get you so far.

As the old saying goes… "what got you here won't get you where you want to go."

> **"what got you here won't get you where you want to go."**

What can in the beginning be the key to success can one day become a set of golden handcuffs.

Be Wary of Glorifying the Wrong Metrics

There is a temptation to glorify hard work as an end unto itself, instead of a means to reaching specific desired outcomes for yourself and your family.

In today's "hustle culture", success is measured not just by results, but by how many hours you put in and how constantly busy you appear. Being 'busy' has become a badge of honor,

and the grind is celebrated as the only legitimate path to achievement.

Social media has amplified this glorification of hustle culture. My experience in various professional groups (dental societies, industry conferences, etc) is often the same. It's tempting to get sucked into playing the wrong game or tracking success by someone else's scoreboard.

In reality, grinding harder doesn't always lead to better results. Many people, even those who achieve financial stability, find themselves emotionally and physically drained. The more you chase the hustle, the more it pulls you away from the things that truly matter—your health, your family, and your overall sense of fulfillment. There becomes a psychological dependency when one's identity becomes tied up being a hard worker or in what you do for a living.

Are You Optimizing For Income or For Time?

At the end of the day, it comes down to one question: Are you optimizing for income or for time? Total dollars earned versus dollars per hour. And why?

> *Are you optimizing for income or for time? Total dollars earned versus dollars per hour. And why?*

Good news: you get to choose.

For example, you might be willing to work 2,500 hours a year to earn $5M, while I'd rather work 500 hours a year and make $2M. It's not the specific numbers that matter, but the relative comparison. What's the value of your time?

For me, the trade-off between that additional $3M and 2,000 hours of free time (40 hours per week) is an easy decision. I had to face this reality over 20 years ago when my daughter was dealing with life-and-death health crises. In those moments, the value of time became far more important than the value of money.

But don't assume everyone's utility function for income is the same. There's no right or wrong answer, as long as your decision is based on your own personal objectives—not societal pressure or limiting beliefs. And over time, those objectives are bound to evolve. Mine certainly did.

In the example above, one person is earning $2,000 an hour, and the other is earning $4,000 an hour. But ask yourself: Are you optimizing for the total dollars earned, or are you focused on maximizing leverage over your time? Would $2M be enough to sustain the lifestyle you want (after taxes) and give you the freedom to invest time in other areas—family, hobbies, creative ventures?

Don't assume it will be. I've seen many high-income earners move the goalposts again and again. What used to satisfy them is quickly surpassed by the drive for more. Honest introspection is essential to determine, "How much is really enough?"

Freedom While You Are Still Young Enough to Enjoy It

Ask yourself—when was the last time you took a vacation longer than a week? Are you still young enough to truly enjoy the adventures, travel, and challenges you once dreamed of?

I've spoken to many overworked dentists over the years who find themselves increasingly disconnected from their families. Despite the long hours they put in to build a better life, they feel they're missing out on the very things they claim to be working toward. Creativity fades, stress becomes constant, and life becomes more about maintaining the grind than about achieving true fulfillment.

There would be nothing more tragic than working your entire life for a certain measure of Freedom only to realize too late that you are too old and no longer physically capable of enjoying it.

> **There would be nothing more tragic
> than working your entire life
> for a certain measure of Freedom
> only to realize too late that you are too old
> and no longer physically capable
> of enjoying it.**

Bronnie Ware captures this vividly in her book, The Top Five Regrets of the Dying. Ware, a palliative care nurse, spent years with patients in their final days and observed recurring themes in their reflections. They didn't regret the money they hadn't earned or the promotions they hadn't pursued. Instead, they wished they'd spent more time with loved ones, allowed themselves to be happier, and lived true to their own values rather than society's expectations. These reflections reveal a deeper truth: when faced with our own mortality, it's time, relationships, and authenticity—not wealth—that hold lasting value. But how often do we pause to ask ourselves if our lives reflect these priorities?

If you truly enjoy the work, the "doing of the thing," that's great. But how much of the "doing" do you really enjoy? Are there aspects you don't take pleasure in that could be deleted, and if so, at what cost? What is it worth to remove from your life an undesired demand on your time? Does there need to be a cost? Is there a better way, and are we simply uncertain and lacking the confidence or guidance to take the risk to enact the necessary change? The hustle culture promises that this is all temporary—that once you reach a certain level of success, you'll have the freedom to enjoy life. Yet, as Ware observed, this "freedom" often arrives too late for many who followed that path. The goalposts keep moving, and the price you're paying keeps going up. And for what? The fulfillment you're chasing feels further away with every passing year.

So, the real question is: Is it worth it? At what point does the cost outweigh the reward? Too many people stay trapped in the hustle, believing that working harder will eventually pay off, without realizing that the very act of pursuit is what's keeping them from the freedom they seek.

Redefining Success: From Hustle to Fulfillment

To redefine success, you need to change how you think about work. Instead of viewing it as a means to accumulate more wealth, start viewing work as a tool to support the things that truly matter—your health, your family, your passions.

True success means not needing to trade your time for dollars, but instead having the freedom to invest your time in what brings you joy. Whether it's spending time with your family, pursuing hobbies, or traveling the world, the ultimate goal isn't to keep grinding—it's to create a life where you control your time.

It's important to recognize that success is personal. There's no one-size-fits-all definition, and there's no need to measure your success against anyone else's. Success isn't about doing more—it's about doing what matters. It's about living a life that's in alignment with your values, your goals, and the things that bring you happiness.

Breaking the cycle of hustle culture and redefining success requires a fundamental shift in mindset. It's not about how much you can work—it's about how much freedom you can create through smarter, more intentional work. Success isn't defined by endless productivity, but by living a life that reflects your values, offers balance, and allows you to spend your time as you choose.

CHAPTER FOUR

Cashflow is King

Using Wealth to Buy Back Time - The Cash Flow vs. Equity Dilemma

Much of traditional "success" wisdom and retirement planning is predicated on the accumulation of assets as a means of measuring achievement and financial security.

I call this, the accumulation of equity. What I have discovered through conversations with hundreds of doctors approaching and navigating retirement, is that you can't eat equity.

It is obvious that some accumulation of resources is required in order to be a successful investor and to prepare for life after your active income years. But that accumulation of assets is not a retirement plan, it is merely the table stakes - a ticket to the game.

Equity must be converted into replacement income.

In order to create income—something we all need—we've

been conditioned to trade our time for money. That's what we're taught to do. We go to school, develop skill sets, and earn degrees or licenses. We're trained to trade our labor and skills for a paycheck, exchanging our time for income. That's the traditional model of how the world works.

For many professionals and business owners, the focus has historically been on building equity. This means accumulating assets like real estate or a business practice, with the long-term goal of eventually selling those assets for a large payout. Equity-building is often seen as the conventional path to wealth, emphasized by financial advisors who encourage the long-term accumulation of assets.

However, the problem with this equity-driven approach is that it's focused on accumulation, not immediate freedom. While equity can provide a large payoff down the road, it typically requires years—if not decades—of hard work, sacrifice, and risk before you can truly reap the benefits. During that time, you remain tied to the grind, working hard to maintain and grow that equity.

Cash flow, on the other hand, offers a different solution. Passive cash flow is income generated regularly without demanding your constant effort. It's the money that flows from rental properties, dividends, or businesses that operate independently of your day-to-day involvement.

> *Passive cash flow is income generated regularly without demanding your constant effort.*

Cash flow gives you the ability to reclaim your time and step away from daily operations. Instead of waiting for some distant future payday, you're creating a lifestyle where your income works for you now.

Equity is still important, and part of building cash flow comes from accumulation—there's no doubt about that. You need to have a certain net worth in the right asset classes to generate sustainable and predictable cash flow. However, in traditional financial models, the emphasis is often placed on equity-building rather than cash flow. While some investments like dividend-paying stocks can provide regular income, the focus remains primarily on accumulation for a future payout.

The difference with cash flow is that it provides freedom in the present, not just the promise of a future payout. The traditional equity-building mindset encourages professionals to accumulate assets, with the hope of one day cashing out. But cash flow offers something more immediate—it's the income that arrives every month, that provides the permission and optionality needed to make changes and buy back your time.

> **Cash flow offers something more immediate. The income that arrives every month, that provides the permission and optionality needed to make changes and buy back your time.**

Building equity is the long-term strategy, but cash flow is what delivers day-to-day freedom. You don't have to wait years for a potential windfall; instead, you create income streams that work for you now, allowing you to step back from the grind and live life on your terms.

The Importance of Balancing Equity and Cash Flow

While building equity is important for long-term financial growth, cash flow offers immediate freedom—the ability to live without being tied to a constant grind. For many professionals, the primary focus is on growing equity, but what's often overlooked is that equity alone won't pay your bills or fund your lifestyle in the present. You need consistent, sustainable income to support your life today.

> *Equity alone won't pay your bills or fund your lifestyle in the present. You need consistent, sustainable income to support your life today.*

Most retirement plans that I have seen over the years place far too much emphasis on equity growth (often in tax deferred accounts such as 401(k)s which have not use prior to a distant retirement "someday") and far too little focus on how to create more Freedom of time now, today, while you are still young enough to enjoy it.

Equity-building gives you assets that appreciate over time, while cash flow provides regular income without requiring your daily labor.

Cash Flow Producing Assets: The Key to Freedom

Real estate is what enabled me to step away from active practice when I most needed to buy back my time. Had I locked up my wealth in a 401(k), I would have been stuck with few options and little ability to make the changes I needed to make to be there for my daughter.

That is one of the most significant concerns that I see over and over again with traditional retirement planning - it is based on an accumulation model and utilizes 401(k)s or other tax deferral strategies that lock up capital for decades and allow for zero optionality in terms of one's ability to create Freedom now, today, without waiting decades or being tied down to the char.

Ironically, not only did that portfolio of income producing assets create the cashflow I needed, but over the years that followed, those assets appreciated in a way that created significant wealth that has allowed my life and options to gradually expand. By diversifying your portfolio with assets that generate cash flow and build equity, you create a financial foundation that not only grows in value over time but also gives you the freedom to step back and live the life you want today.

When you have significant passive cash flow, it allows you to free up your time. And when you free up your time, guess what else happens? Your happiness increases, but also your creativity. Passive income isn't just about financial security—it's about reclaiming your time and, in turn, your freedom.

Why the Accumulation Mindset Keeps You Stuck

Financial advisors and traditional retirement models often emphasize accumulation—saving for the future, building up a retirement nest egg, or creating a massive portfolio of assets to one day "cash out." But this approach has significant drawbacks. The problem with accumulation is that it delays your freedom. It keeps you working, grinding, and sacrificing in the present for a distant future that may never come.

This mindset is deeply ingrained in the way we're taught to think about money and success. The traditional approach encourages the relentless pursuit of "more"—more equity, more savings, more assets—without truly questioning whether accumulating more is what we need to be free.

Part of the problem facing financial advisors and institutions is that when investors are tied to the rising and falling of the markets, it is very difficult to know with any degree of certainty how much is "enough". The default and "safe" answer for financial advisors is to tell their clients to keep working longer and accumulate more.

Without recurring predictable replacement income, it is very difficult to have certainty about how much is enough.

> **Without recurring predictable replacement income, it is very difficult to have certainty about how much is enough.**

The Freedom-Focused Model: Prioritizing Cash Flow for Today

In contrast to the accumulation mindset, the freedom-focused model prioritizes building passive income streams that provide consistent, sustainable cash flow. This model is about shifting the focus from accumulating more to asking, How much is enough? Instead of always chasing the next asset, the freedom-focused model encourages you to think about how much income you need to replace your active work and fund your lifestyle today.

By focusing on cash flow, you can create optionality now, not just in the future. Passive income gives you the ability to replace your earned income without being tied to a job, a business, or the daily demands of running a practice. This shift allows you to stop trading time for money and start enjoying the time you've earned.

The key to the freedom-focused model is understanding that you don't have to wait until you've accumulated a massive fortune to step back and live life on your terms. Instead, by building income streams that work for you, you can begin rclaiming your time right away.

"I just need enough money to tide me over until I need more money to tide me over."

The focus is not just on building wealth—it's on ensuring that wealth works for you, providing you with the lifestyle you want without having to constantly hustle to maintain it.

Shifting Your Focus: From "More" to "Enough"

One of the most significant mindset shifts in moving from the accumulation model to the freedom-focused model is the realization that "more" doesn't always mean better. Many high-income professionals and business owners are stuck in a cycle of always moving the goalposts, constantly increasing their financial targets, believing that once they hit the next milestone, they'll finally be free.

But the truth is, more is never enough. As you accumulate more, your lifestyle often inflates, and you find yourself needing even more to maintain that lifestyle. This is why it's essential to determine your freedom number—the amount of passive income you need to live comfortably without relying on active work. Once you hit your freedom number, you can step away from the hustle, confident that your passive income will continue to support your lifestyle.

Don't assume that everybody's utility function for income is the same as yours. There's no right or wrong as long as you are making the decision based on personal objectives and not because of limiting beliefs or societal pressure.

At the end of the day, building equity is important, but cash flow is what delivers immediate, tangible freedom. It's not about choosing between the two—it's about finding the right balance that allows you to enjoy your life today while still building for the future.

CHAPTER FIVE

Breaking the Cycle

Strategies for Scaling Time

Many professionals, particularly in high-demand fields, start out believing they need to grind harder to reach success. But the real shift happens when you stop being the operator and start thinking like an owner or investor—someone who puts systems, people, and processes in place to generate freedom.

The key is to use work as a tool for building freedom, not as an end in itself. Breaking the cycle starts with delegation and automation. You don't have to do everything yourself. There are countless tasks that drain your energy and time—tasks that can be delegated or automated without sacrificing quality.

Freedom vs Efficiency

Beware the trap of turning your pursuit of Time Freedom into a productivity race. Time management and efficiency are noble pursuits, but real time Freedom will never be found in more aggressive optimization and squeezing more into every fast paced minute. Most successful practitioners are already cramming more productivity into their lives than the average of society. Running faster on the treadmill is not a viable pathway to scaling real freedom of time.

A major paradigm shift is needed. What are the most significant demands on your time right now? How sacred are those obligations? This will require what my wife Kandace calls a "turning of the kaleidoscope" - a willingness to see things from different angles and entertain the idea of making some major pivots in your life.

> ***What are the most significant demands on your time right now? How sacred are those obligations?***

How much would regaining autonomy over your time be worth to you?

Clarifying Decisions

Look for what my friend Blaine Oelkers describes as "Clarifying Decisions" - a decision that eliminates a thousand smaller decisions. Start with the big picture. Choosing to sell your practice by a specific pre-determined date would be a massive clarifying decision that answers a thousand smaller questions.

Clarifying decisions can be large or small. Below are numerous more "everyday" examples.

Clarifying Decisions To Simplify Your Life:

- Utilizing a meal plan service to ensure healthy choices and eliminate countless daily and weekly decisions.

- Hiring a fitness coach to provide an exercise routine and provide accountability.

- Empowering leaders on your team to move forward autonomously within a specific budget or operational scope without needing approval.

- Engaging a laundry service

- Prescheduling annual maintenance

- Establishing a family budget

- Automating bill payments

- Joining a coaching group or program

- Removing social media apps from your phone

Where are their opportunities to make a single decision that allows you to regain more optionality and control over your obligations and time?

This starts with honest introspection and (ideally) conversations with your spouse about goals, desires and hopes.

Delegation - A Hidden Superpower

One powerful way to reclaim your time is by hiring a virtual assistant. While a virtual assistant is only one option for taking items off your plate, it can be transformative. Virtual assistants help with a range of responsibilities, from managing your schedule to organizing communications and keeping projects on track. By delegating these routine tasks, a life changing level of optionality and time freedom can be reached.

If you are serious about scaling Freedom of Time in your life, this is one of the most transformational moves you can make.

If hard work alone were the key to success, then some of the hardest working people in the world would also be the most successful. But that's not the case. Success comes from how effectively you can leverage your time and energy, not just how much you put in.

> ***Success comes from how effectively you can leverage your time and energy, not just how much you put in.***

How To Utilize an Executive Assistant

Make a list of all the tasks you currently do in three columns:

1. Proficient & Passionate
2. Not-Proficient & Passionate
3. Not-Proficient & Not Passionate

Keep doing #1 those make you happy, #2 and #3 offload these

based on what will free up the most time for you. Make a list of Possible Tasks/Projects to assign to an Assistant. Compile a list of best practices/checklists/etc.

Tasks An Executive Assistant Can Help With

- Booking travel – flights, hotels, ground transportation, manage awards programs
- Vendors – research, vetting, coordination, scheduling,
- Business/personal insurance research, comparisons
- Gatekeeper – help you say "no"
- Insurance billing and verification
- Investment tracking & paperwork – filing, storing, cataloging
- Manage communications - email, phone, messages
- Manage calendars – booking appointments, scheduling
- Tax organization
- Spreadsheets / producing reports – all types of bookkeeping
- Providing transportation
- Shopping – gifts, groceries
- Follow-up – pusiness and/or personal
- Writing - articles, books
- Research and recommendations – finding best prices

- Project management
- Creating standard operating procedures (SOPs)
- Finding new employees, associates
- Scanning documents
- Opening mail
- Maintaining supplies
- Running errands
- Tech troubleshooting
- Household repairs
- Ironing / housekeeping
- Yard work / pool maintenance / landscaping
- Meal prep / cooking
- Digital & social media marketing
- Attending meetings for you and taking notes to report back
- Data entry work
- Things you don't like to do for or at the practice
- Any office functions you get dragged into
- Things other people could do better than you

Best Practices For Virtual Assistants

Use Confidentiality Agreements

Ensure that all parties involved sign confidentiality agreements to protect sensitive information, intellectual property, and proprietary processes from being disclosed or misused, fostering trust and legal security in the relationship.

Paying per Hour and/or Paying per Project

Decide whether to pay hourly for flexible, ongoing tasks or per project for clearly defined deliverables, tailoring the payment structure to incentivize efficiency and align with the scope of work.

Start with Small Pilot Test Projects/Tasks

Begin with small, low-risk assignments to evaluate the capabilities, reliability, and fit of the individual or team before committing to larger or long-term projects, ensuring a strong foundation for collaboration.

Use the 10–80–10 Method

Devote 10% of your effort to setting the vision and expectations, delegate 80% of the work to your team, and reserve the final 10% for reviewing outcomes and providing feedback to ensure the project stays on track.

Have High Daily Communication – Daily Email Report

Maintain regular and structured communication through daily email updates, detailing progress, challenges, and next steps to ensure alignment, transparency, and prompt issue resolution.

Services That Offer Executive Assistance (Always Personally Test/Vet Before Use)

- **revaglobal.com/** REVA Global - Use to find real estate-trained virtual assistants.

- **priorityva.com/** Use for high-end executive assistants with founder Trivinia Barber (from my personal network).

- **rocketstation.com/** Use to find real estate trained virtual assistants with founder Robert Nickell.

- **belaysolutions.com/** Use to find virtual assistants, bookkeepers, and web specialists.

- **getmagic.com/** Use to incorporate assistants into your team.

- **zirtual.com/** Trained assistants for business owners and professionals

- **staffvirtual.com/** Offshore outsourcing

- **gsdqueen.co/** Use for guidance to hire for gaining time back. Ashlee Hirschfeld, The Founder, is from my personal network.

You Can Do This

For many of my colleagues, the thought of entrusting someone else with various tasks and activities can seem intimidating. Doctors tend to be perfectionists and like the control that comes from doing it yourself. This is understandable. But what are the tradeoffs? I've spoken with hundreds of doctors about engaging an assistant. Only a small percentage have actually followed through and done so. For those who have, the results have been life changing.

CHAPTER SIX

The Power of Clarity & Focus

Why Most Never Achieve Freedom

In the journey to financial freedom, clarity and focus are your greatest allies. The path to true independence begins with understanding what you really need to live life on your own terms. This is where the concept of the freedom number becomes essential. Your freedom number is the amount of passive income you need to cover your monthly expenses and sustain your desired lifestyle without relying on active work.

Defining Your Freedom Number

We first introduced the concept of the freedom number in the chapter "The Evolution of Freedom," where we discussed its importance in guiding your journey toward financial independence. Understanding your freedom number brings clarity to your goals—it turns a vague desire for "more money" into a concrete target. Instead of endlessly accumulating wealth, you focus on a specific number that, once reached, gives you the freedom to spend your time as you choose.

To define your freedom number accurately, start by listing all your monthly expenses, including:

- Housing
- Utilities
- Food
- Healthcare
- Entertainment
- Travel
- Other lifestyle costs.

This exercise forces you to evaluate your true needs versus wants, allowing you to create a realistic financial target that reflects the life you wish to live. It's about aligning your financial goals with your values, making sure that every dollar of passive income you generate contributes to a life that feels rich in experiences, relationships, and personal growth.

Linking Freedom to Personal Values

Your freedom number is not just a financial metric; it's a representation of your personal values and priorities. It challenges you to think beyond just money, asking instead, What do I want to do with my time? Who do I want to spend it with? What experiences and passions bring me the most joy? Answering these questions creates a powerful connection between your financial goals and the life you truly desire. It's not about striving for endless wealth, but about designing a life that maximizes your freedom, happiness, and fulfillment.

Strategic Use of Assets for Passive Income

Reaching your freedom number isn't just about saving more money; it's about using your assets wisely to generate consistent cash flow. The key lies in strategic investments that work for you, producing income without demanding your constant involvement. Assets like real estate, dividend-paying stocks, or a well-structured business are ideal tools to help you achieve this level of financial independence.

> *Reaching your freedom number isn't just about saving more money; it's about using your assets wisely to generate consistent cash flow.*

Building a portfolio that emphasizes cash flow over accumulation is a strategic move because it allows you to cover your expenses now, freeing up your time to focus on what matters most—whether that's creativity, spending time with loved ones, or pursuing passions that bring fulfillment. The income from these investments acts as a buffer against life's uncertainties, giving you the freedom to make decisions that aren't solely based on financial necessity.

For example, owning rental properties or investing in dividend stocks means you're not just relying on the appreciation of these assets; you're also benefiting from the immediate cash flow they generate. This dual approach—building both equity and cash flow—ensures that while your net worth grows, your lifestyle isn't constrained by a lack of disposable income.

Focusing on Clarity: Shifting from Accumulation to Purpose

One of the most significant mindset shifts when defining your freedom number is moving from an accumulation mindset to a purpose-driven approach. The goal is no longer about how much you can accumulate but about how effectively you can generate the income that gives you control over your time. This clarity helps you prioritize investments and make decisions that align with your values, ultimately allowing you to design a life that's rich in experiences, relationships, and personal growth.

> **The goal is no longer about how much you can accumulate but about how effectively you can generate the income that gives you control over your time.**

The traditional approach to wealth-building often emphasizes accumulation—stacking up assets, building a portfolio, and growing your net worth. But this strategy often leads to more stress and less freedom because you're always striving to hit the next milestone. When you focus on your freedom number, however, you're not aiming for a massive fortune; you're aiming for financial stability that buys back your time and enriches your life.

The Role of Focus: Avoiding Distractions and Staying Aligned with Your Goals

In a world full of opportunities and distractions, focus is what keeps you on the path to true financial freedom. Once you set your sights on achieving your freedom number, it becomes easier to filter out distractions and avoid the temptation to chase short-term gains that don't contribute to your long-term objectives. Every investment you make should be a step toward building a life centered around the things that matter most to you—health, relationships, creativity, and personal fulfillment.

> *Every investment you make should be a step toward building a life centered around the things that matter most to you*

Staying focused means saying no to societal pressures that push you toward traditional models of success that might not align with your values. It's about understanding that real success is not in how much you accumulate but in how much freedom you can create with what you have. This clarity helps you make decisions that are truly aligned with your goals, rather than being swayed by external expectations or short-term gains.

Leveraging Technology for Financial Clarity

Technology can be a powerful ally in helping you stay on track with your financial goals. Using tools and apps to track your income, expenses, and investments can offer real-time insights into your progress toward achieving your freedom number.

Automation of income streams—like reinvesting dividends or setting up automated transfers from rental income—ensures that your assets are always working for you, maximizing growth with minimal oversight.

Balancing Present Enjoyment with Future Goals

Achieving your freedom number doesn't mean you should sacrifice the present for a better future. It's about striking a balance between enjoying life today while still planning for tomorrow. True financial freedom isn't just about living a rich life later—it's about creating a lifestyle now where you can enjoy meaningful moments with family, friends, and loved ones without worrying about finances.

> *True financial freedom isn't just about living a rich life later—it's about creating a lifestyle now where you can enjoy meaningful moments with loved ones without worrying about finances.*

Living in the moment while still being strategic about your future goals means you're not waiting to start living once you hit a certain level of wealth. Instead, you're designing a life that's fulfilling, purpose-driven, and rich in experiences, regardless of your financial milestones.

Dealing with Setbacks and Adjusting Your Freedom Number

Financial journeys are rarely a straight line. There will be setbacks and adjustments along the way, and that's okay. It's crucial to see these challenges not as failures but as opportunities to refine your strategy and stay focused on your long-term goals. Your freedom number may shift over time due to changes in lifestyle, health, or economic conditions, and that's a natural part of the journey to financial independence.

What matters is having the resilience and clarity to adapt when things don't go as planned, and to keep your eyes on the ultimate prize—a life where your income supports the time and activities that matter most to you.

Clarity and Focus as the Path to Freedom

The power of defining your freedom number cannot be overstated. It is the blueprint for a life of true independence—a life where your income works for you, not the other way around. By shifting your focus from merely accumulating wealth to creating passive income streams, you gain the freedom to design a life that prioritizes joy, balance, and purpose.

In the end, it's not about how much you have; it's about how much freedom your income provides. Clarity in your financial goals leads to a life where you're not just surviving but thriving. Your freedom number is not just a financial milestone—it's a gateway to a life where you can invest your most precious resource: time.

CHAPTER SEVEN

Freedom is Just the Beginning

Time as the Ultimate Asset

As we come to the end of this journey, it's clear that true wealth is not defined by the accumulation of assets or the relentless pursuit of more money. It's defined by the freedom to control how you spend your most valuable resource—time. Throughout this book, we have explored what it means to live a life of financial freedom, but at its core, the journey is really about reclaiming your time and using it to create a life of meaning and purpose.

Final Thoughts on Freedom and Time

We've delved into the traps of hustle culture, debated the merits of cash flow versus equity, and redefined success to focus on balance, relationships, and personal fulfillment. The central theme that emerges from all these discussions is that financial freedom is not just about accumulating wealth; it's about using that wealth to buy back your time.

In a world that often measures success by material gains and career achievements, we must remind ourselves that wealth, in its truest form, is about having the freedom to choose how we spend our time. Financial stability is merely a stepping stone to a life where you can invest your hours in the people and activities that matter most. Time is the only resource you cannot replenish or replace, and its value far exceeds that of any monetary gain.

> **Wealth, in its truest form, is about having the freedom to choose how we spend our time.**

Reflections on the Journey to Financial Independence

The journey to financial freedom often begins with ambition—driven by the desire to succeed, to accumulate wealth, and to build a secure future. But as we climb the ladder of success, many of us realize that the higher we go, the more distant our original goals of happiness and fulfillment seem to be. This is where clarity and focus become crucial.

Financial freedom is not a destination; it's a state of mind. It's about breaking free from societal expectations that equate busyness with success and shifting your perspective to see wealth as a tool to enhance your life, not dominate it. True freedom is found when your income supports the life you want to live, not the other way around.

Call to Action: Reflect on Your Relationship with Time and Wealth

As we conclude, it's important to reflect on your relationship with both time and wealth. Here are some key questions to consider as you move forward:

- Are you living a life that aligns with your deepest values and goals, or are you caught up in the endless pursuit of more?

- What are you truly working towards, and is that goal worth the time and energy you're investing in it?

- Have you clearly defined your freedom number—the amount of passive income that would allow you to live comfortably and on your terms?

The call to action here is to redefine your approach to success. Move away from the relentless grind that prioritizes wealth accumulation over life experiences. Instead, focus on designing a life where your financial goals support a lifestyle of joy, purpose, and balance. This shift is not just about a change in strategy; it's about a transformation in mindset—a declaration that you will no longer sacrifice your most valuable asset, time, in exchange for fleeting gains.

Leveraging Financial Strategies for Time Freedom

Throughout this book, we have emphasized the importance of leveraging financial strategies that create passive income streams—investments that allow your money to work for you so that you can step away from the daily grind. This approach is about more than just building a safety net; it's about creating a sustainable lifestyle that you can enjoy today, not someday in the distant future.

Investing in tangible assets like real estate, dividend-paying stocks, or automated businesses is not just a strategy for wealth accumulation; it's a way to regain control over your time. By focusing on these types of investments, you move beyond the paycheck-to-paycheck cycle and into a realm where your income flows steadily, regardless of whether you're actively working or not.

Imagine a life where your days are no longer dictated by the need to make ends meet, where your time is spent creating, exploring, and connecting rather than grinding for financial gain. This is the life that strategic investments can help you build—a life where financial security provides the platform for personal growth and fulfillment.

> ***Imagine a life where your days are no longer dictated by the need to make ends meet, where your time is spent creating, exploring, and connecting rather than grinding for financial gain.***

The Redefinition of Success: Purpose Over Profit

As we explored in previous chapters, the definition of success is changing. It's no longer about the size of your bank account or the prestige of your title. Success is now being measured by the quality of your life—how much time you have to spend with your loved ones, the depth of your relationships, and the joy you find in your everyday experiences.

For too long, the traditional model of success has celebrated the hustle—the idea that the harder you work, the more successful you'll become. But we've seen that this mentality often leads to burnout, strained relationships, and a sense of emptiness even at the peak of financial achievement. True success is about balance; it's about knowing when to push forward and when to step back to savor the fruits of your labor.

Purpose-driven success means aligning your financial goals with your personal values. It's about asking yourself not just, "How much money can I make?" but also, "How much freedom can I create?" This shift in focus is what transforms financial goals from a never-ending chase into a journey that enhances every aspect of your life. For an inspiring approach to making the most of the time you have with loved ones, I highly recommend 18 Summers by Jim and Jamie Sheils. Their book offers a thoughtful framework for prioritizing family time and creating meaningful experiences, reminding us that we have only a limited number of summers with our children and loved ones.

The Legacy of Time Freedom

In the end, what you leave behind is not the wealth you accumulated or the accolades you earned. It's the impact you made, the relationships you nurtured, and the time you devoted to the things that truly mattered. Your legacy is defined by how you spent your time—how present you were with your loved ones, how much joy you found in your daily life, and how fully you lived the moments that make up your life.

Time is the ultimate currency, and how you choose to spend it will determine the quality of your legacy. As you move forward, remember that financial wealth is a tool, not the end goal. Its purpose is to create the space and opportunity for you to live a life that is rich in meaning, connection, and joy.

Designing a Life of True Freedom

Designing a life of true freedom means making intentional choices that prioritize your happiness, health, and relationships over the relentless pursuit of more. It's about crafting a lifestyle that allows you to be fully engaged in the present moment while still planning for a secure future.

> **Designing a life of true freedom means making intentional choices that prioritize your happiness, health, and relationships over the relentless pursuit of more.**

The decision to focus on passive income and defining your freedom number is not just a financial strategy—it's a commitment to a life where you control your time. It's the ultimate act of taking ownership over how you live, love, and contribute to the world around you.

Final Reflection: The Ultimate Measure of Success

As you close this chapter, ask yourself: How will you measure your success? Will it be by the money you earn, or by the freedom you gain to live life on your own terms? Will it be in the number of hours you worked or in the quality of the moments you created?

True wealth is not about what you accumulate but about what you experience and how deeply you connect with the world around you. It's about the laughter of your children, the adventures you take, the people whose lives you touch, and the peace you find within yourself.

Let this journey be a reminder that your time is your most precious asset. Guard it, cherish it, and use it to build a life that is not just about surviving, but truly thriving. Because in the end, time is not just money—it's the very fabric of life itself.

AFTERWORD:

What Is Freedom Founders?

Freedom Founders evolved organically from my own experiences creating personal financial freedom in my early 40s. In the years that followed my practice sale, colleagues began privately confiding with me, wanting to know how I was able to exit practice mid-career without financial constraint. I began to guide and teach some of the frameworks I had learned through my own experience.

Fast forward to today, Freedom Founders has become my "Next" and my primary avenue of creating impact and significance. This is a group and community of high-income professionals who are working together to achieve financial security, passive income, and diversified wealth through strategic real estate investments, tax-efficient wealth-building strategies, and collaborative networking opportunities.

It is a place for personal transformation — home for the misfits who refuse to buy into the conventional life model offered by society and sold by most financial advisors.

We curate real estate investments better than any other group that I am aware of, but what many find when they become a part of the community is that real estate is only a vehicle by which one can create the life you truly desire.

With the right frameworks, investing is the easy part. The real challenge comes from embracing freedom in each area of one's life and finding the permission and the courage to build the life you really want.

DIY vs. Done "With" You.

Most real estate groups and education out there is geared towards one of two outcomes:

1. Making you a landlord.

They send you out into your local neighborhood to find deals, orchestrate the project, dealing with contractors, tenants... I call this becoming an "accidental landlord."

This could be a viable path for a young person with more time than money (it is the path that I took before I had a practice or a family). But at a certain point in your career, you begin to desire a path that does not require starting from scratch or reinventing the wheel. Is it possible to fold time and climb on the shoulders of those who have gone before?

2. Selling you specific deals.

The reality is that most real estate groups are commission-based and designed to sell investors into specific deals in which the group facilitators are often GPs (General Partners in the deal) and stand to profit significantly from selling their own projects.

Through our reputation and my decades of experience, I curate and bring together a network of relationships that provide access points to investment opportunities in a variety of real estate asset classes. I do not have any financial interest in where our members choose to invest.

It's All About Community!

1. Community and Mentorship.

Freedom Founders offers a supportive community and mentorship network specifically designed for high-income practitioners. The community provides a space for like-minded individuals to collaborate, share experiences, and gain insights and guidance on wealth creation and passive income strategies.

2. Financial Independence and Wealth Building.

The community is centered around the pursuit of financial independence and achieving sustainable wealth through strategic investments. We aim to empower members to take control of their financial futures and leverage their professional success to build diversified income streams, particularly through real estate.

3. Education and Resources.

We provide members with access to educational resources, proprietary content, and expert guidance in real estate investing, tax-efficient wealth building, asset protection, and legacy planning. The community offers a wealth of knowledge and insights tailored to the unique financial situations and career paths of high-income professionals.

4. Strategic Real Estate Investing.

Real estate investing is a cornerstone of our wealth-building philosophy. We guide members through learning about passive income generation, cash flow optimization, leveraging tax advantages, and diversifying real estate portfolios to create long-term wealth.

5. Legacy Planning and Asset Protection.

We also address elements of legacy planning, asset preservation, and risk management in long-term wealth building. Members gain access to guidance on estate planning, asset protection, and succession planning to safeguard and transfer generational wealth.

The Freedom Founders Community serves as a comprehensive platform that equips high-income professionals with the knowledge, resources, and support needed to pursue financial independence, build sustainable wealth, and create passive income streams. Through our focus on real estate investing, tax-efficient strategies, and community engagement, we give our members a pathway to achieve long-term financial security and fulfillment.

Ready To Learn More?

Whenever you're ready, here are additional resources and ways I can help fast-track you to your journey to freedom of time, money, relationships, health, and purpose.

Other Books I've Written That Dive Deeper:

Own Your Freedom: Sustainable Wealth for a Volatile World, by Dr. David Phelps with Dan S. Kennedy.

OwnYourFreedomBook.com

What's Your Next?: The Blueprint For Creating Your Freedom Lifestyle: FindYourNext.com

The Apprentice Model: A Young Leader's Guide to an Anti-Traditional Life: ApprenticeModelBook.com

Inflation: The Silent Retirement Killer: How to create security amidst new economic realities: InflationBook.com

From High Income To High Net Worth: Alternative Investment Strategies to Stop Trading Time for Dollars and Start Creating True Freedom: HighIncomeBook.com

Get your Retirement Scorecard:

Benchmark your retirement and wealth-building against hundreds of other practice professionals and business owners. Get personalized feedback on your biggest opportunities and leverage points. Go to FreedomFounders.com/Scorecard to take the three-minute assessment and get your scorecard.

Listen to my Podcast:

I post weekly interviews and monologues that explore the topics of this book and more — How practitioners can become their own financial advocate amidst today's economic volatility and uncertainty.

Listen in at: DentistFreedomBlueprint.com

Schedule a call with my team:

If you'd like to replace your active income with passive investment income within two to three years, and you have at least $1 million in available capital (can include residential or practice equity, business equity, whole life insurance and retirement accounts), then visit the following link to schedule a call with my team. They can help explore potential alignment and help you discover your pathway to freedom: FreedomFounders.com/Discover.

Thank you for reading, and I look forward to helping you achieve Financial Freedom!

Dr. David Phelps, DDS

Who Is Dr David Phelps? and Why Should You Listen To Him About YOUR Money?

A PRACTICE OWNER TURNED CEO AND LEADER

David owned and managed a private practice dental office for over twenty-one years before his daughter's health crisis served as a dramatic wake-up call in his life. David's "Plan B" (a portfolio of cash-flow producing real estate assets) gave him the Freedom to sell his practice mid-career and focus 100% on what matters most to him.

David is a renegade, he does not follow the majority but lives life and does business on his own terms and is not dictated to by others.

AMERICA'S #1 AUTHORITY ON CREATING FREEDOM IN LIFE AND BUSINESS

David is the author of 6 published business, finance and success books. As a nationally recognized keynote speaker, David brings dynamic energy and rare insights into how to create financial freedom through passive income, how to build a real business that doesn't take over your life, anti-traditional real estate investing, private lending, wealth-building legacy, and how to take responsibility and "own" your life.

A LEADER BORN THROUGH CRISIS

Sitting with his daughter in the hospital room after her battle with leukemia and a life-saving liver transplant, Dr. David Phelps realized what matters most. It was not his career as a dentist that had consumed his daily life for over twenty-one years. He needed to be present for his daughter Jenna.

He decided he would no longer practice dentistry. Instead, he developed his "Plan B."

He drew inspiration from his years of investing avidly in real estate that began in dental school with a joint-venture with his father. By leveraging the lessons and capital he had acquired, David built an investment portfolio that could generate enough passive income to leave his dental practice and be the father his daughter needed.

ESCAPING TRADING TIME FOR DOLLARS

David's radical new life intrigued his peers, who asked him how they too could command control of their wealth and time. By bringing together his two worlds—high-income medical professionals and real estate professionals—David created a powerful network of like-minded professionals who could support each other on their own paths to financial and personal freedom.

He called this group Freedom Founders, and as its leader he found his purpose: helping his colleagues break the chains of enslavement to their practices and financial fears and create freedom in their lives.

With his own life as proof, David challenges the traditional model of wealth building, which preaches abdicating control over one's money to advisors and entrusting all of one's investing capital to Wall Street.

David has witnessed too many high income professionals blindly trust the traditional path only to have their hard-earned wealth wiped out by the volatility of the public market. Through Freedom Founders, David exhorts his members to take back control of their investing capital from their practices and 401(k) plans, put it to work in more stable, capital producing assets like real estate, and always stay focused on their freedom.

YOUR NETWORK IS YOUR NET WORTH

Freedom Founders Mastermind Group began as a meeting of sixteen people over a decade ago and has grown into a community of over one hundred forty members and Service Providers, where his insights into the financial markets, alternative investing, as well as achieving success and fulfillment in life bring members from across the country.

Speaking from his own experience, David strives to instill in his members the courage to lead lives unhindered by the expectations of others and driven by purpose. Following in his footsteps, Freedom Founders members attain the tools to become Free for Life: they can live entirely on the passive income from their real estate investments.

A RECOGNIZED LEADER IN DENTISTRY AND REAL ESTATE

David has been featured in Advantage Forbes Books, The Profitable Dentist, Dental Success Today, The Progressive Orthodontist. He has been awarded the GKIC Marketer of the Year.

David regularly collaborates with countless industry leaders including Dr Dustin Burleson, Dr David Maloley, Steven J Anderson, Scott Manning, Alastair Macdonald, Dr Scott Leune, Dr Annisa Holmes, Dr Christopher Phelps, and many others.

At his own events, he has shared the stage with Garrett Gunderson, Chuck Blakeman, Adam Witty, Tony Rubleski, Thomas Blackwell, and others.

AN EXPERT IN THE WORLD OF REAL ESTATE

David's expertise in the world of real estate includes everything from multi-family apartments, self-storage, commercial properties, retail properties, single-family rentals, structured notes, private debt, managed funds and more. He has successfully weathered multiple market corrections - notably using the 2006-2008 downturn to successfully more than double his net worth.

He is regularly consulted in the creation and management of large multi-investor syndications and funds secured by real estate assets.

www.ingramcontent.com/pod-product-compliance
Lightning Source LLC
LaVergne TN
LVHW012034060526
838201LV00061B/4599

www.ingramcontent.com/pod-product-compliance
Lightning Source LLC
LaVergne TN
LVHW012034060526
838201LV00061B/4599